Dedication

To my parents, Hy and Martha Larris, thank you so much for the loving home you created for my brothers and me. Growing up, we were incredibly fortunate to have your strong marriage as our foundation. Wherever I go your values and life lessons go with me. So do my sweet memories of you both.

To my David and our extraordinary children Fayette and Ezra, you three are, and always will be, like a handprint on my heart. And to Vermont: You da dawg and we all miss you.

Acknowledgments

As Middle School Confidential continues, so does my gratitude to Judy, Jenni, Janell, and the rest of the incredible Free Spirit team. You all possess a winning combination of warmth, social consciousness, and professionalism. Special shout-outs go to: Michelle Lee whose innovative graphic design leaps off every page, turning text into fun; to Matt Kindt for caring so much about "the kids" and each artistic detail of their inner and outer lives. From cover to cover, you rock. And to Douglas Fehlen, my continued appreciation for your open mind and impeccable sense of organization and tone. Because of you, every book in this series is better in every way. Thanks also to Marin County librarians Holly Stanalan and Shereen Ash, my point women for recommended teen reads.

Because this book is about family, I want to acknowledge my brother Alan. Thank you for the sensitivity and support you gave so freely after Dad died. Because of the solid ground you provided when I was 15, I was able to move forward with confidence. Thanks also to my brother Don for the laughter, for your caring heart, and for turning me on to *The Twilight Zone*, Bob Dylan, and *Mad* magazine.

I want to thank my daughter Fayette, always fearless in life, in love, and in curries. You've always inspired me. To my son Ezra, my favorite debate opponent and kitchen companion. I can always count on you for the truth. Fay & Ez, write on! To my soon to be daughter-in-law Sarah, having you in our family is a gift.

And finally, to my husband David, my best friend, favorite geek, and partner in all that I do. Here's to 35 years of love and family.

Contents

BOOK 3

What's Up with My Family?

MIDDLE SCHOOL CONFIDENTIAL™

ANNIE FOX, M.Ed.

free spirit
PUBLISHING®

Library of Congress Cataloging-in-Publication Data
Fox, Annie, 1950–
  What's up with my family? / Annie Fox.
    p. cm. — (Middle school confidential series ; bk. 3)
  Includes index.
  ISBN 978-1-57542-333-3
  1. Teenagers—Family relationships. 2. Teenagers—Psychology. 3. Adolescent psychology. 4. Parent and teenager. I. Title.
  HQ796.F749 2010
  646.7'80835—dc22

                                                                    2009029476

At the time of this book's publication, all facts and figures cited are the most current available. All telephone num-bers, addresses, and Web site URLs are accurate and active; all publications, organizations, Web sites, and other resources exist as described in this book; and all have been verified as of September 2009. The author and Free Spirit Publishing make no warranty or guarantee concerning the information and materials given out by orga-nizations or content found at Web sites, and we are not responsible for any changes that occur after this book's publication. If you find an error or believe that a resource listed here is not as described, please contact Free Spirit Publishing. Parents, teachers, and other adults: We strongly urge you to monitor children's use of the Internet.

Reading Level Grades 6 & Up; Interest Level Ages 11–14; Fountas & Pinnell Guided Reading Level Y

Edited by Douglas J. Fehlen
Cover design and illustrations by Matt Kindt
Interior design by Michelle Lee

10 9 8 7 6 5 4 3 2 1
Printed in China
P17201209

Free Spirit Publishing Inc.
217 Fifth Avenue North, Suite 200
Minneapolis, MN 55401-1299
(612) 338-2068
help4kids@freespirit.com
www.freespirit.com

Introduction

Hi. I'm an online advisor at a Web site for teens (www.thesite.org). A lot of the email I receive is about family issues. "How can I get my parents to quit being overprotective?" "What do I do to win back my mom's trust?" "I have the most annoying brother (or sister) in the entire world!"

Every once in a while teens will disagree with adults at home and siblings will drive each other crazy. Okay, it probably happens more often than that, but the point is, it happens . . . *in every family.* It's normal for family members to have trouble getting along all of the time. But normal doesn't have to mean *necessary.* If you need some new strategies for making peace at home you've come to the right place.

In addition to the usual clashes of personality and opinion, serious issues can also come up in families. Parents might fight a lot and eventually separate or divorce. Maybe you've experienced other tough family situations—like getting used to life with a stepparent, facing the loss of a loved one, or dealing with money or health issues at home. Perhaps you'd just like to feel closer to the people you live with but you don't know how.

No matter what's up with your family, you can find out a lot in these stories about six teens dealing with their own challenges at home. You'll also find quotes and advice from real teens, quizzes, tips, and insider tools for doing your part to make your family happier and stronger. If you have any questions that aren't addressed in this book, feel free to email me at help4kids@freespirit.com. I'd also enjoy hearing any stories or suggestions of your own.

In friendship,
Annie

P.S. I often use the word *parents,* but the advice here can help whether you live with one or two parents, a stepparent, a foster family, an aunt or uncle, grand-parents, or other people. When you see the word *parents,* just think of the adults you live with—that's who I'm talking about.

We were at Jack's house waiting for Jen,
when Mateo's phone rang....

We know that no family is perfect. Jen hardly ever agrees with her parents about anything. Abby's fed up with her mom's "helpful hints" about losing weight. Jack can't stand how his sister gets away with everything. Mateo feels like his huge family is always in his business. Michelle would love to have a family bigger than just her and her mom. Chris, on the other hand, wants it just to be him and his mom again because with a new stepdad and stepbrother, it's not the same.

At times, we've all wished things were different at home, but none of us had a clue how to change what we don't like. Then Michelle asked one of her famous probing questions:

ASSUMING THAT EVERYONE'S GOT AT LEAST ONE FAMILY COMPLAINT, WHY NOT ASK OTHER TEENS HOW THEY DEAL?

So we asked. And we learned some really useful stuff that we wish we'd known sooner. But better late than never. And lately, things are better.

Michelle

Chris

Abby

It's pretty common for teens to feel like adults at home are too strict or controlling. Maybe your parents or other family members also have a way of checking up on you that makes you think they're overprotective. It might seem like they see you as untrustworthy and requiring 24/7 supervision. But more likely, they just aren't used to the fact that you're getting older and becoming more responsible.

It's natural for the people who raise you to have some trouble getting out of the habit of treating you the way they did when you were younger. Back then it was all about protecting you from danger or harm. And it still is. Only now it can seem like too much because you're more independent and able to figure out a lot of stuff on your own. That's when constant questions and concerns about what you're doing might get on your nerves.

From the "Give Me a Break" FILES

"My mom and my stepdad help out at my school on different days so they have lunch with me twice a week. I love them and all, but I think that's too much."
—Sasha, 10

"My mom treats me like I'm eight! She thinks I should never be awake past 10:30 and always uses that tired excuse, 'I don't care what other parents let their kid do.'"
—Peter, 13

"I caught my grandma in the movie theater lobby asking them to make sure that I was there!"
—Asif, 12

"My dad says, 'When I was 13 I had biked across most of my town!' But my mom won't let me bike one mile!"
—Nicholas, 13

"My parents don't think I should talk to boys on the phone, so they're always trying to catch me doing it. How can I get them to understand that I'm too old to be treated like a baby?"
—Dani, 14

"I stayed after school to watch my friend try out for soccer, and I didn't have access to a phone right away. I called my stepmom later and she yelled at me. When I got home I found out that I was grounded."
—Julio, 11

"My friend lives with her aunt and uncle. They don't trust her, even though she's really responsible. She's never allowed out and it upsets her."
—Claudia, 13

The Inside Scoop About Overprotective Adults

Does having an overprotective parent mean you're a troublemaker or someone who has to be watched over night and day? Of course not. Sometimes it's more about them than about you. Knowing *why* adults at home feel the need to be constantly in your business can help you gain more independence. Here are some possible reasons:

1. **They are worriers.** Some adults worry more than others. An overactive imagination can make it hard for them to relax. If you live with one or more worriers, your safety probably isn't the only thing they fret about. Try talking through their concerns.

2. **They aren't always sure of themselves.** Adults are sometimes more nervous with the first (or only) child in the family. Why? Because for every new phase you reach they are trying to decide what new rules you need to stay safe. Letting them know that you understand where they're coming from can help them see you're capable of making good decisions.

3. **They haven't yet switched gears.** As a little kid you needed an adult directing your every move. Fast forward to the present: You're getting older, but the adults who have raised you may not have figured out how to parent the new, more mature version of you. You're going to have to be patient with them as they learn how to deal with your becoming more independent.

4. **They need reassurance.** Every time you show the adults in your family that you can make responsible choices you help them calm down, worry less, and feel better about giving you more independence. You might think of every new responsibility as a test of whether you're ready for more freedom—pass and you can move up to the next level of trust.

Parents are hardwired to protect their kids. And that's a good thing. If animals didn't care for their young and keep them away from predators, those babies wouldn't survive long enough to reproduce. If that happened across an entire species, we're talking about extinction!

So parenting is about protecting the young ones until they can protect themselves. Of course, not all animal parents protect their kids as intensely or for as long as humans. Some reptiles, for example, don't bother at all. There are snakes, fish, and lizards that actually *eat* their own babies. (Disgusting, but true!) **And when it comes to people watching over their children, there are differences from family to family.**

HUH! PARENTS SOMETIMES GET IT RIGHT.

"I actually needed that . . ."

"I was feeling depressed about school and stuff with my friends. My grandma tried to get me to talk to her. I wouldn't so she kept bugging me to talk to the counselor. Finally I did and I actually felt better."
—Kaylie, 12

"My youth group was going to Washington, D.C. I didn't really like any of the guys in the group so I decided not to go. My dad talked to me about what a cool opportunity it might be, but he said he'd respect my decision either way. I decided to go and I'm really glad. It was amazing!"
—Reggie, 14

"I failed a class at school because I spent too much time playing video games with friends. My dad and I had a big and very serious talk. Thanks to him, I fully learned my lesson. Now I am proud of him and myself."
—Zach, 13

"I was going to have sex with my ex-boyfriend. We were moving really fast. My mom found out and she was so mad and scared, she made me break up with him. But I am glad she did. I would have lost my virginity and regretted it. I could have gotten hurt emotionally, too. I am happier than ever and I am thankful my mom did that."
—Raven, 14

"My mom said I couldn't spend the night at my friend's because she didn't trust one girl who was going. Next day I find out that bad stuff happened. Stuff like people getting drunk and other things that I would never do in my life. I'm thankful my mom said I couldn't go because if I went, I would have regretted hanging out that day."
—Sasha, 13

5 TIPS FOR GETTING MORE RESPONSIBILITY

1. Keep your promises. Whenever you make an agreement with your parents, follow through. This shows that you can be counted on. When they trust you, you earn more independence. You also gain self-respect—that's win-win.

2. Look for more ways to help out at home. Adults appreciate it when everyone in the family lends a hand. Want to earn bonus points? Do something that's not one of your regular chores just to help out. Parents love that!

3. Get along with siblings. Do your part to make the peace with brothers and sisters, and adults may notice something has changed for the better. In their minds, getting along equals maturity. And maturity gets you more responsibility.

4. Try to have a positive attitude. It's not like you have to smile and act 100 percent happy all of the time, but cooperating with adults at home will make them more likely to cooperate with you. That's just the way it works.

5. Show family adults they've done a good job raising you. When you ask for new freedom and meet your responsibilities head-on, you prove to your parents that you've learned what they taught you. That makes them proud. It should make you proud, too.

People often see what they want to see and hear what they want to hear. We're all guilty of getting so caught up in our own thoughts that we miss what's going on with someone else. For this reason, it can help to remember that parents are hardwired to protect you. (Where have you heard that before?) Instead of feeling frustrated with rules that seem designed to keep you from doing what you want, try talking to adults at home about how they decide what you can and can't do. You might begin to understand their feelings better and be in a better position to work together on a solution that makes everyone happy.

WE'RE WORKING
IT OUT

"My grandparents would get really worried when I went out, but I would always call them so they knew I was okay. Soon they started to feel more trust in me and they didn't worry anymore. You just have to make sure you are always honest, even when it's hard."
—Byron, 11

"At home, go above and beyond what you have to do without being asked (for example, fold the laundry or clean the living space). Don't argue, complain, or act frustrated when asked to do a task. Just these simple steps alone will work wonders when trying to gain parents' trust and respect. It's really not that hard."
—Michael, 12

"When I was 12 I got invited to a party that lasted until 11:00 p.m. I'd never been out that late before without my family, so my mom sat me down and asked me questions like, 'What would you do if someone offered you something and you didn't know what it was?' Then my mom let me go to the party because she believed I would be responsible."
—Katy, 14

"I kept telling my parents, 'I'm growing up,' and they finally got it! Now I'm allowed to go out with my friends as long as I tell my parents in advance. I can also go for a walk whenever I feel like it."
—Angel, 13

Need to Know?

100 Things Guys Need to Know by **Bill Zimmerman.** Part graphic novel, part practical advice, this book for guys has information for handling all kinds of tough situations—including ideas for earning more privileges and getting along with adults at home.

It's My Life—Family
www.pbskids.org/itsmylife/family
Visit this Web site for the lowdown on topics that cause challenges in families. Find suggestions on everything from communicating with parents and siblings to dealing with a family move and other transitions.

Real Families: Figuring Out Your Family and Where You Fit In by **Amy Lynch.** Families have their good moments, but some other times aren't so fun or easy. This book for girls features ideas for dealing when adults at home have issues with friends, dating, and other topics.

It's normal to feel annoyed with adults in your family if they sometimes treat you like you're much less mature than

you are. If you're patient and follow their rules, though, they should eventually get with the program. Because the truth is, adults at home don't want to be checking up on you forever. But they won't feel ready to step back until they believe you've proven you're ready to make more of your own decisions.

So that's the deal. The more you can show adults at home that you're responsible, the more they'll relax and see that you're ready for more freedom.

You probably know a lot of insider information about your family—like everyone's favorite TV shows or least favorite foods. No doubt you also have an idea of what makes each person happy, embarrassed, or stressed. And the people in your family probably know all these same things about you. Knowing each other so well is part of what makes families feel connected.

Unfortunately, family members don't always do the best job of using what they know. During conflicts or high-stress times people might say stuff just to upset one another. Or someone may make a random comment that really hits a sore spot. Maybe family members don't mean to hurt anyone's feelings. They might not even realize they've said anything wrong. But whether they meant it or not, thoughtless remarks can sting and make it seem like people at home don't care about how you feel. Maybe someone is in a bad mood and you just happen to be there. Or maybe a sibling has an annoying habit that you've never mentioned, but one day you've had enough and you lose control. At those moments respect and trust might go missing in action, and what's left may not be a pretty sight.

HEY! DON'T MY FEELINGS COUNT?

GUESS I'M NOT THE ONLY ONE WITH HURT FEELINGS.

"My aunt and grandma make comments about personal things. They know it bothers me, but they keep doing it."
—M.J., 11

"My sister calls me bad names. When I say stuff back to her, my mom only yells at me and not her."
—Lynnette, 12

"My grandparents pay more attention to my sister than me. I don't want to make it into a big thing, but they ought to treat us the same, right?"
—Carla, 13

"I'm a vegetarian, and every time my dad makes meat I can smell it. It makes me sick. I've asked him to please stop, but he just says, 'Too bad.'"
—Arno, 13

"My mom keeps guilting me into going to family parties with her fiancé because his kids came to one of ours. I told her that I have friends and family members of my own. She called me inconsiderate and selfish. Why can't she try to understand where I'm coming from?"
—David, 14

"My twin brother makes me so angry. He tells his friends embarrassing and untrue things about me. I cry and then he laughs at me! My mom and dad think I'm just being dramatic, but I'm not!"
—Rose, 12

"My parents always ask me to do stuff with them. Maybe they like going on hikes, but I'd rather be on the computer or watch TV. Why can't they respect that?"
—Jerry, 14

MOVING Past Hurt FEELINGS

The next time it seems like your family isn't respecting your feelings, tell yourself, "What I'm complaining about is real." Seriously. If you feel like the people in your home don't get where you're coming from (or don't care), on some level you're probably right. Unfortunately, feeling sorry for yourself won't help the situation. Here are some things that can:

1. **Identify your feelings.** The first step to making changes is telling yourself the truth about what's really going on inside. For example, "I feel frustrated when I'm telling my mom something and she acts like it's not important."

2. **Think about what you can do.** Thinking about what everyone else should do or stop doing isn't going to magically improve your situation. You can only control your own actions, so whatever solution you come up with will have to start with you.

3. **Ask yourself:**

   — What do I need to be happier right now? (Respect? An apology? A chance to speak my mind? Forgiveness? Some fun? Peace and quiet? Someone to talk to?)

   — How could I do a better job asking family members for what I need?

   — How could I do a better job getting what I need from friends?

   — How could I do a better job giving myself more of what I'm looking for?

A comment, a not-so-funny joke, an out-and-out insult . . . they are all just words. But depending on who said what, words can bring you down. Suppose, instead of letting go of what was said and moving on with your life, you start thinking: "No way am I going to let him get away with that!" "Mom loves her more than me." "Does everyone feel that way about me?" Just like a snowball getting bigger as it rolls down a mountain, fuel-ish thoughts can turn a random comment or a rude remark into a lot of anger, jealousy, or worry.

Fuel-ish thoughts can shake your confidence and drag you down into negative thinking. They can also build walls between you and a family member or you and a friend. All that can be going on in your mind, even if no one actually meant to hurt you in the first place.

"Can't stop thinking about it . . ."

"My mom's getting married and she didn't even ask me how I felt about it! I don't like the guy. I tried talking to my mom but she won't listen. She thinks everything will go smoothly when she gets married but it won't. I just know it!"
—Ted, 12

"I think my stepbrother would have nothing to do if he didn't make my life miserable. I know he's trying to be mean and I shouldn't pay any attention to him. But when he says stuff like, 'No one would ever want you for a girlfriend,' I start worrying that maybe he's right."
—Brenda, 13

"My brother has been making comments about me and my weight. I'm not even overweight, but I don't like the way I look. How do I get rid of those thoughts and become satisfied with who I am?"
—Alana, 13

"I had the stupidest argument ever with my parents just for wearing a shirt that was wrinkled. Do they have the right to argue about it? Was it that serious to them? I'm still so angry I keep thinking about it."
—Isaac, 11

"I told my cousin that I had a headache. He said that wasn't normal and that I might have a brain tumor. He wasn't kidding! And since then, I've noticed these weird pains in my neck, but I'm afraid to tell my mom."

Is it
Fuel-ish Thinking?

1. The next time I see him, he'll be so sorry. **Y or N**
2. She's the one who started it! **Y or N**
3. No problem. **Y or N**
4. I just know this is going to be really bad. **Y or N**
5. Let's talk about something else. **Y or N**
6. That's okay. We're cool. **Y or N**
7. My sister is so annoying! **Y or N**
8. No one in this family cares about me. **Y or N**
9. I guess maybe I didn't handle that the best way. **Y or N**
10. I'll talk to him about it, after I calm down. **Y or N**
11. This stuff always happens to me! It's so unfair! **Y or N**
12. I'm such a loser. **Y or N**
13. Huh. I guess he really was just kidding. **Y or N**
14. She said that about me? I'm telling Mom. **Y or N**
15. No worries. I forgive you. **Y or N**

Answers:

1. **Y** Planning revenge keeps you angry.
2. **Y** Blaming can create distance between people.
3. **N** Saying "no problem" and really meaning it is helpful for calming down.
4. **Y** Imagining things turning out badly feeds worries and fears.
5. **N** Changing the subject can put the brakes on fuel-ish thoughts.
6. **N** Making the peace can help dial down the heat in conflicts.
7. **Y** Bad-mouthing someone keeps anger, resentment, and jealousy alive.
8. **Y** Feeling sorry for yourself can add to feelings of sadness and loneliness.
9. **N** Owning up to the part you've played in a conflict can help to work things out.
10. **N** Taking a break with a plan to make the peace later is smart thinking.
11. **Y** Thinking of yourself as a bad luck magnet is fuel-ish.
12. **Y** Talking trash about yourself is guaranteed to make you feel worse.
13. **N** Seeing things for what they really are can help you feel better.
14. **Y** Getting involved in drama can heat things up quickly.
15. **N** Letting go of anger through forgiveness gets you moving toward feeling better.

To make peace after a family conflict, some people say, "Just forgive and forget." But that's not always easy, especially when feelings have been hurt. Even if you're not ready to forgive or forget, it's often best to try to move on. To do that, it can help to stop blaming others and letting go of the feelings that are making things difficult between you and another person.

Why move on? Because letting go of anger, hurt, and resentment can make you feel better. The point is not to forget what's happened, but to stop dwelling on the negative so you can see what's right with a relationship and work to improve things.

Give Some Forgiveness

Forgiving people isn't always easy—especially in situations where you feel someone has treated you badly. Whenever you do feel ready, though, these steps can help.

1. Think of something you're blaming a family member for.

2. Write the person's name on a piece of paper along with a description of what she or he did that bothered you.

3. For each incident, freeze-frame your memory on the moment that upset you.

4. Take some slow deep breaths and think: *At that moment I felt _____ because _____. That moment is past. Over. I choose not to blame _____ for that anymore.*

5. Rip up the paper and toss every bit in the trash.

Completing these steps for any family conflict can help you get over resentment and feel closer to the people you live with. If something is still bothering you, it's a good idea to talk directly with the person.

CHILD'S POSE

Making peace in your family begins with making peace inside yourself. When you're calm, you are in a better place to talk about things and work them out. This simple yoga pose can help quiet fuel-ish thoughts and put you in a better mood. In spite of its name, this pose is good for people of any age.

1. Put a large towel or blanket on the floor.

2. Remove your shoes and socks and kneel on the towel.

3. Sit back on your heels, separate your knees and touch your big toes together.

4. Rest your arms at your sides. Inhale. Then exhale and slowly lean forward, lower your belly on to your thighs and rest your forehead on the towel. Close your eyes.

5. Release any tension in your neck and shoulders and gently press your tailbone toward your heels. Continue breathing.

6. Relax your mind. Imagine yourself resting in a place where everyone loves you and accepts you just the way you are.

7. When you're ready to come out of the pose, put your palms on either side of your knees and slowly push up into a kneeling position. Open your eyes. Stand up slowly.

THIS LOOKS WEIRD, BUT IT FEELS GREAT.

"I PASS ON FUELING UP"

"I was getting angry and making up situations in my mind. Like imagining my parents speaking to me in a nasty way and me reacting in different mean ways. I was just making up a problem in my head that didn't exist. When I realized my mind was taking me on a roller coaster ride, I did some breathing to calm down."
—Kelly, 13

"When I'm totally fed up with my mom, stepdad, or anyone else in my family, I play my guitar. I fool around with some chords until a melody comes into my head. The next thing I know, I'm making up a new song and have forgotten what I was even mad about."
—Taralyn, 13

"Rather than get too worked up about what's going on with my parents, I read a book, see a movie, listen to music, or focus my energy on school."
—Ian, 12

"If I have a big argument at home, I usually take a break and go out— either alone or with a good friend who can relate. I kind of 'renew' myself before going back into the situation. Sometimes I'll pray about it."
—Kevin, 14

"I try to look at the bigger picture and realize that fights with my brother (or whoever) aren't important compared to everything else that's going on in the world. I might also take a walk or go for a run to clear my thoughts."
—Luis, 14

Need to Know?

Bounce by **Natasha Friend.** Life's tough enough for Evyn, whose mom died so long ago she can barely remember her. Things don't get easier when her dad remarries (without consulting Evyn) and she has to live with six new people who don't seem to get her.

Tangerine by **Edward Bloor.** Paul is visually impaired, but that doesn't keep him from seeing all of the problems with his family, his new neighborhood, and the school that won't let him play on the soccer team—even though he's the best goalie around.

TeensHealth
www.teenshealth.org
TeensHealth features advice for dealing with inconsiderate people, hurt feelings, and other tough aspects of life in a family. Also visit this site for information on health and suggestions for staying physically and mentally strong.

Misunderstandings happen in every family because people who live together sometimes say things that cause hurt and anger, whether they mean to or not. You can't control other people's behavior, and you can't always prevent conflicts. But no matter what's going on in your home, you do have control over how you respond. When you pay attention to what you're feeling and notice your mind fueling up, you can choose to stop, calm down, and think about positive solutions. **By getting back in control of fuel-ish thoughts, you are taking a powerful first step toward helping your family get along better. You might also be teaching the rest of them a thing or two.**

With every family, there will be times when situations at home change and things get shaken up (a little or a lot). Maybe parents begin to fight and split up temporarily or for good. A stepparent might become part of your life and leave you trying to figure out where you fit within a blended family. Other events—like a long-distance move or a parent losing a job—can also lead to major changes in the family.

The tough part about these situations is that you probably didn't have anything to do with why they happened. Even so, you have to deal along with everyone else. Change isn't always easy for people. **It can be especially hard if things are moving fast and it feels like you don't have much control over what's going on.**

"Things are different now . . ."

"My grandma died last month. Sometimes I just can't believe she's gone. She was my mom's best friend, so it's affecting her the most. It's hard for my sister, my brother, and me to see Mom so sad."
—Juan, 13

"My dad just moved back in with us after being gone for two years and it has turned my world upside down."
—Bibi, 12

"I'm stressed because of my parents' divorce. It's hard because of the scheduling."
—Raj, 11

"We just moved here and I hate it. My new school is terrible because it is so strict. Now my parents are splitting up, too."
—Aiden, 13

"I just found out my mom is pregnant! They already have my little sister and me. I'm so angry because things are going to have to change again and I don't want them to. Plus they're planning on making my sister move into my room with me so the baby can have its own room!"
—Cheri, 14

"I like my mom's fiancé, but things are moving really fast. They've been together less than two months—it's a lot for me to take in."
—Wallace, 12

"Recently my dad went into rehab and I'm going through a lot right now. It's weird, too, because I'm living with my grandparents and I don't really know them."
—James, 11

How Flexible Are You?

1. **Your family just moved to a new town. You:**
   a) assume that you're going to hate your new school.
   b) blame your parents for ruining your life.
   c) decide to make the best of it and see what happens.
   d) refuse to unpack and give everyone the silent treatment.

2. **Your new stepsister asks to borrow a sweatshirt that you don't wear any more. You:**
   a) let her borrow it.
   b) refuse because you don't want her to get in the habit of borrowing your stuff.
   c) say yes even though you don't totally trust her yet.
   d) make a deal—she can borrow it if you can see her playlist.

3. **Your aunt and her kids moved in with your family. You don't know for how long. You:**
   a) silently resent the extra people, the noise, and the lack of privacy.
   b) tell your parents how you feel.
   c) stay away from home as much as possible.
   d) retaliate against your cousins.

4. **Your stepmom is more particular about keeping things neat than your mom. You:**
   a) leave stuff around just to annoy her.
   b) clean up partway but leave the rest.
   c) complain to your friends about her.
   d) talk to your dad about the situation.

5. Your dad hurt his leg. He can't go to work and may lose his job. You:

a) worry about whether your family will have enough money.

b) resent that he gets to sit home and watch TV all day.

c) ask how you can help the family.

d) pretend you don't care when you really do.

Answers:

1. c. An open mind and a positive outlook can help smooth a rough transition.

2. a. Kindness helps newly blended families bond.

   d. Another smart move that lets you expand your playlist while keeping the peace.

3. b. Communicating about tough situations can help everyone weather the storm. You'll get information you can use to deal with what's happening.

4. d. In a new living situation, it may take time to get used to everyone else's way of doing things. Talking through rules can prevent them from becoming big issues.

5. c. Working together helps families grow stronger during times of change.

Stay Out of
FIGHT MODE

Not knowing how to react to a new family situation can lead to stress, anger, and feeling out of control. Try these tips for staying calm and cool during times of change or conflict:

1. **End aggressive arguments.** When anger spirals into insults, threats, or name-calling, peaceful solutions are hard to find. If it seems like someone is about to go on the attack, get out of there. It may not be easy, but stepping away from tense situations is often the best way to avoid major blowups.

2. **Park insults.** If someone pushes your buttons, there's no law that says you have to react. Angry responses rarely help and often makes things worse. Instead of revving up fuel-ish thoughts, park any insults you were thinking and leave them unsaid.

3. **Give yourself some space.** Putting distance between you and a heated situation can help you figure out your next best move. With a calmer approach and new point of view, your ideas are more likely to help make the peace, not expand the war.

4. **Do something you like.** Taking time to enjoy yourself can help you get out of victim mode. If you like the outdoors, go for a hike. Or ride your bike. Shooting baskets works, too. So can plugging into music and dancing your tail off. You get the idea. It's all good as long as it's safe and healthy.

Big family changes—including separation, divorce, and remarriage—can create challenges for everyone. Money problems, a family move, and other major events can also make things a lot different from the way they were before. Of course, if you're dealing with these kinds of changes now, you already know how hard it can be. Adults in the family may be so focused on what they need to do that it seems like you're alone in dealing with the fallout of what's happened. But people at home probably do want to help—even if that's not always so obvious. And family members, close friends, cool teachers, counselors, coaches, and other people you trust are also willing to listen and help out.

Going through family transitions can be easier if you remember that feeling off-kilter is temporary. Even when something bad has happened, things don't have to stay that way forever. Usually things settle down after a while. New routines and family traditions can really help everyone start feeling more normal again.

When It's Time to Get Help . . .

In dealing with family changes, it's important to get the help of someone you trust right away if you:

- feel worried or afraid about something going on at home.
- are overwhelmed by sadness, hopelessness, or anger.
- want to hurt yourself or others.
- are using alcohol or other drugs, or thinking about it.
- feel out of control or like you might do something you regret.

If you're not comfortable talking with an adult at home, a teacher or counselor, or any other adult in your life, you can call the Nineline (1-800-999-9999)—a 24/7 helpline for teens.

NEED A NEW Approach?

Dealing with changes (and challenges) at home can be tough—especially since all family conflicts are not the same. It can help to find the right approach for each situation.

Approach #1: Assertive—respectfully telling people how you feel

Try it: Suppose your stepbrother messed with your stuff. If you two have a history of talking things out, then telling him how you feel can work well. *Result?* Being assertive helps others understand where you're coming from and what you expect of them.

Time to reconsider: When adults at home are upset, they may be in no mood to hear what you have to say. That's when being assertive may look like disrespect. *Result?* Adults might get angrier. You may want to try another approach or use this one once they've calmed down.

Approach #2: Passive—letting others take the lead without arguing or resisting

Try it: If other family members are yelling at each other, it may be best to stay out of it. *Result?* Not adding fuel to the conflict might allow everyone to cool down sooner.

Time to reconsider: If you don't like the way you're being treated, staying passive and quiet can prevent others from understanding how you feel. *Result?* The (unfair) treatment is more likely to continue.

Approach #3: Peacemaking—looking for a compromise

Try it: When neither side is willing to give an inch, peacemaking can offer a new approach. *Result?* You might help the family work together so everyone gets some of what they want.

Time to reconsider: If family members are not ready for a compromise, they might turn against you. *Result?* Your good intentions may temporarily create more conflict. Even if they're not listening yet, staying calm can help others settle down, too.

5 TIPS FOR DEALING WITH CHANGES

When life at home changes, hoping things return to the way they used to be isn't going to get you to a better place. As you look to the future, it can help to remember that change isn't necessarily all bad. Here are some ways to help yourself adjust.

1. **Focus on the positive.** Instead of missing the way things used to be, focus on the good stuff in your current life. Like the fact that you and the people you live with are *still family*.

2. **Create new family traditions.** If you're living with someone new, new traditions can help jump-start your life together as a family. It could be as simple as a regular movie or game night.

3. **Make new friends.** If you're in a new community or school you're going to need new friends. Join after-school activities. Let your interests guide you.

4. **Join a youth group or the Y.** Most cities and towns have lots of stuff going on. Find out what's going on in your neighborhood by reading newspapers, checking bulletin boards, or going online.

5. **Check out the library.** Libraries have much more than just books. Many are comfortable places where you can hang out, read, use computers, and listen to music.

"MY LIFE 2.0"

"Whatever you do, don't blame yourself for problems your parents may be having. Do not! It's not your fault if they don't want to be together anymore."
— Riley, 12

"If parents fight to the point that it is too much for the kids to see, it's better if they don't live with each other anymore. Just because they don't love each other anymore doesn't mean that they don't love you."
— Shireen, 12

"My mom had a drug problem and now she's in rehab. My two sisters and I live with my grandma. It's really different here and there's a lot I don't like, but I'm grateful that my grandma is taking care of us. Still, I hope my mom gets better."
— Rick, 14

"My dad started having problems at his work, so we moved. It's as if my great life just melted away. At first I couldn't stop thinking about all the stuff I was missing. But then I got into a band and met a few cool people. Also, my dad got another job. Now things are definitely better."
— May, 13

"A year ago, our family went on vacation and my uncle and I got sick. I got better but my uncle didn't. He died of pancreatic cancer a few months ago. The whole family still misses him and all, but we're not as sad as we were. So I guess we're doing okay."
— Edgar, 12

Need to Know?

Families Change
www.familieschange.ca
Visit this site for information on divorce, separation, and other transitions that may be affecting your family. Find answers to a lot of tough questions that can come up when life at home is changing.

Including Alice **by Phyllis Reynolds Naylor.** After years of being the behind-the-scenes matchmaker for her dad and her favorite teacher, Alice believes all her dreams will come true when they finally get married. But after the wedding, life isn't as Alice imagined and she has to figure out where she fits in this updated version of her family.

Stuff: The Life of a Cool Demented Dude **by Jeremy Strong.** Fourteen-year-old Simon, known as Stuff, struggles to keep the peace at home when his dad's girlfriend and her daughter move in.

Life in your family today may not be the way it was before. Changes happen, whether you vote for them or not. Sometimes you can see the changes coming and you have time to get used to them. Other times they might occur without warning so that the ground seems to shift under your feet. Finding your footing again can be really tough.

It can help to remember that you're not at fault for what's happened. And there's nothing you can do to magically put everybody on their best behavior. But you can control how you respond to what's going on, which includes bringing the right attitude to a situation. Will everything always work out perfectly? It won't, but you'll be in a better position to deal with whatever is around the corner.

Family blowups can be triggered by all kinds of situations, but things can really heat up when it seems like adults are being unfair.

Maybe they're against certain music or clothing styles. They might have different ideas about how much is "too much" when it comes to texting, playing video games, or watching TV. Or maybe their objections are more personal, like not trusting particular friends because they're "bad influences." Then there's dating—which parents and teens often have a difference of opinion on.

Whatever the issue, it often comes down to adults believing you're not ready to do something when you're sure that you are. It can be hard when they don't seem to think you can make your own decisions. Because of frustration on both sides, big arguments are pretty common. But just because something is common, doesn't mean it's the best approach. Adding anger to these situations can lead to things spiraling out of control with hurtful things being said. What's worse, shouting and the rest of it is useless in getting what you want since it shuts people off from each other. If no one is really listening, nothing gets worked out.

From the "UNFAIR!" FILES

"I don't know how to get across to my dad that when I 'argue' I'm just trying to show him my point of view. When he insults me I want to defend myself, but I just can't. I feel really helpless."
—Phil, 13

"My parents say I am too young to be in a serious (or unserious) relationship and that this boy I like is not allowed to call me anymore. They said they are being more protective of me than my brother because I am a girl. That really bothers me!"
—Leigh, 13

"No makeup, no laptop, and no music. No camera, no low tops, no short skirts, and no texting. No going out with my friends and no boyfriend. My life feels like a freaking prison."
—Sylvia, 14

"I want to play football, but my parents won't sign the permission slip. My brother messed up his knee playing, so now I'm not allowed."
—Kevin, 11

"It's midterms and I'm earning a failing grade in Spanish. My parents have threatened to move me to another school—meaning they would be taking away the few friends I have. I'm so mad at them right now."
—Walt, 12

"My dad makes me so angry sometimes. He always thinks he knows what I am thinking. I just want to yell at him and tell him he doesn't get it. But instead I nod my head and roll my eyes. Both ways I get in trouble."
—Bethany, 12

Dealing with Unfairness

It can be tough staying cool when someone pushes your "unfair" button, but you can learn how. Up for the challenge? Try this:

1. **Notice what's going on with you.** When you start feeling like you're losing control your chest may tighten. Your mind may start filling with fuel-ish thoughts.

2. **Stop.** Slam on the brakes before you go off the deep end and do or say something that's going to get you in trouble. Even if you've already said or done some things that weren't great, it's never too late to stop.

3. **Close your eyes.** Closing your eyes blocks out the person you're angry with and helps you get back in balance faster.

4. **Breathe.** Inhale *slowly* and evenly through your nose. Then relax your mouth and exhale *slowly*. Repeat 5–10 times.

5. **Decide.** Now that you're calmer, think about the best way to respond to what happened.

6. **Your challenge.** From now on, whenever you start to feel like you're losing it, remember to breathe and put yourself back in control.

Does It Run
in the Family?

If the adults in your family set limits that make no sense to you, then getting more information can help you understand where they're coming from. Think about the following questions:

"Why is this the rule?" Your parents have reasons even if you don't know what they are. By asking calmly and respectfully, they are more likely to take your questions seriously and give you straight answers. You may not agree with what they say, but at least you won't be clueless.

"How were you raised?" There's often a connection between the kind of parent an adult becomes and the kind of parents he or she had. For example, if you're not sure what kind of parents your grandparents were, then ask. Most family histories are filled with interesting stories and clues to help you better understand adults from generation to generation. (See "Collecting Life Stories" on page 69.)

"What kind of parent would I like to be?" If some day you have kids the same age as you are now, how much freedom would you give them to make their own decisions? What family rules would you have? Why do you think that kind of parenting would be good for your future children?

Even when you understand where parents are coming from, you may still believe their rules are unfair. It can be pretty frustrating when adults at home have made up their minds about something and seem to ignore anything you have to say about it—even when you have good points to make.

When decisions or rules don't seem to make sense, it can be pretty tempting to go ahead with whatever it is you wanted to do. The problem is that this can only make things worse at home. First, parents are probably going to find out—if not right away, then sometime later. That's going to lower their level of trust in you and make it less likely you'll get what you want the next time around. Another thing: No matter how right you think you are about something, being secretive will strain relationships. Even if adults don't realize what's going on, *you're* going to know the truth. That can feel pretty bad and create distance between you and other people at home.

Here's What I'm Going to Do

HMMM . . . THESE DON'T SOUND LIKE REALLY SMART PLANS.

"My parents won't let me go with my girlfriend to a party at my friend's house because they think we might have sex or do drugs. I wouldn't do that! But I still want to go, so I'm thinking I'll just say we're going somewhere else."
—Theo, 14

"I speak my mind and don't like it when my family treats me unfairly. I get A's and help around the house. I have friends, and I'm in two music programs. What do they want? I know that running away is hard, but I'm afraid I'll crack from this pressure."
—C.J., 11

"My parents blocked the account for my Web page, so I'm going to figure out a way to access it using my friend's account."
—Li, 12

"My school has a big annual dance. Most girls leave early to get ready. I'm not going to the dance, but I'm thinking of leaving to hang out with my boyfriend until 2:30 when, like always, I go baby-sit at my older sister's house. There's no way my mom can find out I didn't spend the whole day at school."
—Traci Lynn, 13

"My parents let me have only one sleepover a week. I don't understand it! They might not trust me, but I can make good decisions on my own. With this whole one night thing, I can't hang with friends tomorrow night or the next! I'm desperate, so my friends and I are going to come up with something."
—Tanya, 13

WANTED:
Permission to . . .

Going behind the back of adults at home is a bad plan for getting more independence. There is no surefire way to make adults see your side of things, but sometimes the way you ask for permission — and how well you follow through — can help improve your chances:

1. **Be honest.** Present all the facts concerning what you want permission for. If you want to go to a movie, don't say it's PG when it's actually PG-13. Fudging the facts, even if it seems like a little detail, can sabotage your efforts.

2. **Give them a reality check.** If your friends have already gotten permission from their parental units based on the facts (see #1), yours may feel more comfortable with the plan. Encourage them to talk with the other adults. It may not work, but it's worth trying.

3. **If they say no, ask for an explanation.** Talk to them calmly and respectfully and listen to their objections. It's not going to help to interrupt or cop an attitude. Really listen to what they're saying. Remember what usually motivates them . . . (yes, the safety thing).

4. **Offer a compromise.** For example, if they say "no way" to you and your crush going alone to a movie at night, ask permission to go during the day with a group of girls and guys. No guarantees they'll agree, but when you show willingness to compromise, adults may meet you halfway.

5. **Be 100 percent trustworthy.** If they say, "Call us when you get to your friend's house," don't argue and don't flake. Just call. If they say, "Come home by 9:00 p.m.," walk in the door no later than 8:59. Respect their rules and there's a good chance you'll get more independence.

How Do YOU Feel?

If a sibling, cousin, friend, or anyone else you care about is doing something unsafe, it's important you take action to help. Talk with the person, telling him or her what you know and why you're worried. If a situation is serious, or if you've spoken with the person and nothing changes, silence is not an option. It's important to talk with an adult at home or someone you trust at school. Remember: It's not ratting—it may be saving a life. The person you're worried about may get mad, but the most important thing is that they're safe. Don't be afraid to call 911 in emergencies. That's what it's for.

GETTING THROUGH AN Apology

Blowups in families are never a good idea, but they do happen. This can be a chance for all to see that the way you and your parents have been talking to each other may not be working very well. At this point, your power comes from the fact that you can always begin moving in a healthier direction.

1. **Understand what you did.** If you're not sure, then ask. Put all your excuses aside and listen until you understand why your parents are upset.

2. **Apologize sooner than later.** Any time you make a sincere apology, you're doing the right thing. But stalling allows bad feelings and mistrust to build walls between you and family adults, which can make apologizing become that much harder.

3. **Be real.** We all make mistakes and do things we regret—it's a sign of maturity to own up to them. Speak the truth and say it like you really mean it. Copping an attitude or blaming someone else misses the whole point.

4. **Do it face to face.** Looking a family member in the eye and saying, "I'm sorry" shows respect for the person.

5. **Be specific.** For example, "I'm sorry I said you are the world's worst parents. I was just trying to hurt you" is a first class apology. "Hey, I'm sorry you were upset by what I said" is a first class cop-out.

6. **Make a plan.** Think about what you'll do next time and make sure you don't cancel out your apology with future actions.

Need to Know?

Estrella's Quinceanera **by Malin Alegria.** As the family gets carried away planning her quinceanera (a traditional 15th birthday celebration), Estrella starts dreading it. Where does she fit between the world of her barrio and her rich private school friends?

The InSite
www.theinsite.org
Visit this site for tips you can use to get along with family members while standing up for yourself and what you believe. There are suggestions you can use to get more of what you want more of the time—all while working with (instead of against) adults at home.

The How Rude! Handbook of Family Manners for Teens: Avoiding Strife in Family Life **by Alex J. Packer.** Getting along at home isn't always easy—especially when you and adults have different ideas of what should be okay. This book features ideas for keeping the conversation civil and building more trust at home.

At times it can seem like adults at home have all the power—with unfair rules and total control over your life. But the truth is that you have power, too, and it lies in the day-to-day choices you make. Your actions can build trust with family adults and help you negotiate for more responsibility. Keeping your word and keeping your cool—even when you disagree—will go a long way toward showing them you deserve the independence you want.

How a person feels may not always be obvious, though sometimes it is. When people feel down or stressed, even if they don't come right out and say it, they're often sending signals. For example, you probably can think of time when someone in your family was upset and you got the message from his or her tone of voice or body language. Maybe the tip-off was that the person overreacted to some small thing. Bad moods are no fun to be in or around . . . but we've all been there at one time or another.

So what triggers bad moods? It could be anything. Maybe it's problems with friends, boyfriend/girlfriend issues, or something else that doesn't go right at school. Maybe you come home feeling fine and get "infected" by someone else's bad mood. No matter how a mood starts, when someone is in one, even minor disagreements can turn into major blowups.

I Don't Feel Like BEING NICE

"I really liked this girl at my old school but then my family moved 500 miles away! I'm in a bad mood and I'm fighting with my whole family all the time."
—Jacob, 13

"My grandma sometimes tells me, 'You have the worst attitude in the whole world.' And when I'm being pretty rotten, I think she's right."
—Adell, 12

"People tease me and I'll get mad inside, but on the outside I act like I'm happy. Getting teased always puts me in a terrible mood. Sometimes I do take it out on my family."
—Cecile, 13

"Sometimes I'll go days without talking to my parents and being very flippant when I do. My dad gets very angry and tries everything to get me to talk to him."
—Martin, 13

"I just yelled at my stepdad and stepsister for complaining about my dog eating some food he wasn't supposed to. I'm really angry because I'm sick of hearing complaints about my dog."
—Reggie, 12

"My mom will twist my words to make it seem like I'm treating her so horribly. She always makes the excuse that she doesn't feel good because she has fibromyalgia. Like that makes it all right."
—Viv, 12

Bad Mood Trigger?

1. You're doing your own thing when your aunt says you have to baby-sit for your little cousins tonight. **Yes, No, Maybe**

2. The adults at home don't know that you broke up with the person you were going out with. They ask, "How come we haven't seen you two together for a while?" **Yes, No, Maybe**

3. Your dad promised to drive you and your best friend to the movies, but now he says he can't. **Yes, No, Maybe**

4. You're supposed to meet up with friends, but your grandmother reminds you that you haven't finished your chores. **Yes, No, Maybe**

5. Your sister gets into your room and messes with some of your stuff. **Yes, No, Maybe**

6. Your mom makes a meal you can't stand and says you have to eat it. **Yes, No, Maybe**

7. You work hard on a science project and your baby stepbrother wrecks part of it the day before it's due. **Yes, No, Maybe**

8. Your uncle asks about a test that you didn't do well on. **Yes, No, Maybe**

9. Your sister says she saw your crush talking with your best friend. **Yes, No, Maybe**

10. You get a birthday gift that you really don't like. **Yes, No, Maybe**

Answers:

7–10 Yes or Maybe Answers. Changes in plans and disappointments have the power to trigger bad moods. Noticing when the mood switch gets flipped and figuring out what might have caused it can help you put on the brakes and get back to feeling okay.

4–6 Yes or Maybe Answers. From time to time, all of us get into a bad mood because of something someone else did or said. When this happens to you, you usually don't hang out in that mad or sad place for long because you're learning how to brush it off.

0–3 Yes or Maybe Answers. No one is happy all the time, but everyday disappointments or frustrations don't often get you down. When you do get thrown off balance, you usually know how to get back in the game quickly.

4 TIPS FOR BATTLING BAD MOODS

1. **Identify mood triggers.** Suppose your mom complains (again) that you haven't cleaned up your "mess." The nagging triggers a bad mood. Instead of arguing and turning this into a bigger mess, you could try picking up after yourself without being told. Sure it means extra effort, but at least the nagging and the mood it triggers are history.

2. **Notice physical signs and give yourself space.** If, for example, someone at home makes a random comment that upsets you, your heart may start racing. Or you might feel a knot in your stomach. That's normal when you're angry or stressed. Instead of taking it out on the other person, take a break from the situation. You could try a breathing or relaxation exercise (see page 28) to help you calm down.

3. **Plan your way out of a mood.** If your parents won't let you do something, your frustration may lead you to thinking of ways to get around their rules. Usually these are bad ideas that will only create more problems for you. Instead, make a plan that will let you work with adults at home to get more of what you want. Page 14 has some ideas for doing this.

4. **Take a break.** Whenever you feel a bad mood start, with fuel-ish thoughts piling on, you probably need a break. So go ahead and take a walk, take a shower, or take a nap. Get a snack, get some exercise, or plug into some music. Lose yourself in a book, play a game, or call a friend. As long as it's safe, it's cool. Afterwards you'll be in a better place to deal with whatever is going on.

Now and then everyone gets stuck with a negative attitude. When that happens, we may know something's going on with us but not why. Other times we know exactly why we're in a bad mood but we're not sure if we want to get unstuck. Part of us may wish we could flip the switch on angry feelings and make peace with the people around us. But another part may actually want to hold on to the negative attitude—even if it's not really working for us.

Family members spend so much time around one another, it's easy to get into conflicts where small, unimportant things become a big deal because no one wants to back down. Other times real worries about family situations can fuel bad moods.

It's Hard to Get UNSTUCK

"My mom has a boyfriend and I'm scared they'll get married and I won't be important any more. Lately I've been nasty to her. I even asked her, 'Why do you like him? He is boring and looks like a hairy wart.' That hurt her feelings. I know I shouldn't say that stuff, but how can I not?"
—Leeza, 12

"I am known in my family for my inability to snap out of a bad mood."
—Kathy, 13

"I have a very big attitude problem at home. It's like I can't say anything without getting grounded. I wish I was one of those people who can just laugh things off."
—Owen, 14

"It's not fun for me to be awful to my mom, but I am just so angry with her over so many things, I want to release it any way I can."
—Jeannie, 11

"I argue with my parents almost every day about picking up after myself or chores. I'll admit it—sometimes I'm disrespectful to them. I don't mean to be, and I always say I'm sorry. But then I kind of do similar stuff the next day."
—Tyronne, 12

"I tell myself that I should be old enough to say, 'Okay, being quiet and making dirty faces at my mom and sister are not going to make me feel better.' But I just can't snap out of it. It's like I don't know what to do with myself."
—Simon, 13

How to
Get Unstuck

1. **Pay attention to how you're feeling.** A quick change in mood can be a warning sign that you're becoming frustrated. The quicker you notice a negative mood, the easier it is to get back to feeling right again.

2. **Think about where the mood has come from.** Think back and locate the moment when you started to feel this way. For example, imagine you're playing a video game or IMing a friend and suddenly your mom says, "Please take out the trash now." Could that have kick-started your bad mood?

3. **Be on the lookout for fuel-ish thoughts.** Maybe after hearing your mom you think: "I hate when she interrupts me. Like what I'm doing is never important. Like I don't deserve respect!" These kinds of thoughts can get you stuck even deeper.

4. **Tell yourself the truth about what you're doing.** Sometimes people use a negative attitude to punish other people. Being honest with yourself can make you stop and think. "Yeah, it's true. I'm acting like this to get back at Mom and make her feel bad. Hmm. Is that really what I want to do?"

5. **Try to drop it.** It's not always easy, but it might be easier if you admit that what you're doing isn't working, "This is making me look really immature—not actually what I was going for." If you still feel stuck, move on to #6.

6. **Take some slow deep breaths.** Breathe in and think, "I am breathing in a better mood and attitude." Breathe out and think, "I am letting go of anger, hurt, and frustration." Repeat the cycle five times.

MOVING PAST MOODS

"I am pretty much always aware when I'm in a foul mood. I write poetry and that helps me get into bad feelings and release them."
—Leon, 14

"I usually take time out for myself on the weekends so I get 100 percent relaxation. Everyone needs to have alone time at least once a week—especially if you have a big family like I do. You'll feel better and your mind will, too."
—Karl, 13

"At night I lay in bed listening to music. When I hear musicians being honest and putting their thoughts out for the world to hear, it helps me. There are a few singers who know how to put into words exactly the things I feel. Listening to them always makes me feel better."
—Mac, 14

"When I need a break from family stuff, I take a nice hot shower, read, study, organize my room, whatever. I know people who hate every single one of these activities, but I enjoy them a lot. They also put me in a better mood to be with my family again."
—Paulette, 13

"For me, it's really relaxing to sit in our attic in front of the cooler and meditate. It's dark and the cooler is loud so I can't hear anything else. I clear my mind of my bad mood."
—Nikki, 12

MAKING CHANGES

Families are all about relationships and interactions. Your parents or siblings say things and you react. You say things and they react. Patterns can quickly become habits—for better or for worse. Getting out of bad habits isn't always easy, but you can try this:

1. **Fold a piece of paper in half.** On one side write, I wish my parents/siblings would _____ more. On the other side write, I wish my parents/siblings would _____ less.

2. **Complete each sentence.** You probably have lots of opinions, so go ahead and write them all down.

3. **Look over both lists.** Which are the three most important items? If your family became more of what you want and less of what you don't want, how would your life be different?

4. **Talk to your family members.** Show the lists. Ask what they'd like more of and less of from you. (Hey, it's only fair.)

5. **Family experiment.** For one week, work on one "more" item and one "less" item from each other's lists. See what happens. If no one is willing to join in, make changes based on the feedback you got. Even if just one person in the family became more cooperative, it could have a positive effect on everyone's attitude.

Need to Know?

If a Tree Falls at Lunch Period **by Gennifer Choldenko.** Two kids. Two lives. The challenge of a new school for one. For the other, the challenge of parents who seem to be on the verge of splitting up. But when Kirsten and Walker become friends, they find new strength to handle hard times.

TeensHealth
www.teenshealth.org
This site features health information and recommendations for staying physically and mentally strong. A lot of the suggestions relate specifically to stressors that come up at home, including arguments with parents, divorce, and other tough situations.

No family has perfect understanding and communication 24/7. It's impossible because people are naturally going to have different responses to what's going on each day. Add to this mix everyone's changing moods and attitudes and things can get challenging (and confusing) in a hurry.

No one has the power to alter someone else's mood or behavior, but working on what's going on with you can help make things go more smoothly at home. At the same time, trying to understand why others are reacting a certain way can be really useful. **Each person in the family, after all, is part of a team. Working together can help you come up with solutions that work for everyone.**

Unfortunate things happen in every family. That's just the way it is. A bad situation has the potential to change every part of how you live your life. This can be especially true when people you care about are no longer there all the time. Maybe a divorce takes one parent away for long periods. The death of a family member might leave you feeling lonelier than ever before. Or maybe someone you love isn't literally gone from your life, but a health condition or another situation prevents the person from being there for you in the way you need. Your family may have faced some major troubles recently. Or perhaps something happened long ago that still comes back to you—like aftershocks following an earthquake.

"PART OF MY FAMILY IS MISSING . . ."

"My mother is facing depression. She stays in bed all day and keeps telling me how lucky she'd be if she died."
—Dionne, 13

"My father is a raging alcoholic. He's never been there for us."
—Sonya, 14

"Not having my dad around is hard and my mom doesn't make it any easier. Sometimes I wish that my family were like most of my friends' families. But it will never happen."
—Kyle, 13

"My uncle is in jail for selling drugs again. My dad is really angry with him and my grandma is crying all the time. It feels like my family is falling apart."

"My aunt and uncle weren't legal so they got deported. My cousins are living with us for now, but we're not sure what's going to happen with them. It's unfair that we can't all be together like before."
—Said, 12

"My sister and me were best friends until she moved in with her boyfriend. My mom and stepdad aren't talking to her and she never answers my texts! It somehow seems like she's died."
—Cathryn, 14

"Two days ago my dog got hit by a car and died. I can't get over the fact that my best buddy isn't here. And to make matters worse, he died when I was with him. I saw him all busted up by the car. It was actually a drunk driver."

True or False?

1. When both parents live together, families are definitely happier. **T or F**
2. When someone close to you dies, the pain and sadness never go away. **T or F**
3. If parents get in trouble with the law, their kids have no chance of success. **T or F**
4. If parents abuse alcohol or drugs, their children are to blame. **T or F**
5. Kids raised by a single parent always have serious problems. **T or F**
6. When parents split up, it's usually the kid's fault. **T or F**
7. If a parent is depressed, it's because of the stress of having children. **T or F**
8. Being raised in foster care is not as good as living in a "regular" home. **T or F**
9. Parents who don't live with their children never think about them. **T or F**
10. When a grandparent is really sick, there's not much kids can do. **T or F**

Answers:

1. False. Happiness comes from having family members who care about one another—no matter who they are or where they live.

2. False. Loved ones who die are always remembered, but the pain of the loss can fade with time.

3. False. All people make their own choices and create their own futures.

4. False. People who abuse alcohol and drugs are responsible for their actions, not anyone else.

5. False. Some teens of single parents have problems and some don't. Some teens with two parents have problems and some don't. With people, there is no "always."

6. False. Parents split because they have relationship problems. Kids don't cause those.

7. False. Depression is a mental illness. No one causes it.

8. False. A real home is any place you live where there are people who care about you.

9. False. Absent parents may think about their children often. Other reasons may prevent them from staying in touch.

10. False. During the illness of a family member, acts of kindness and love are always helpful.

MISSING
Someone?

1. **Honor your feelings.** Whether you're experiencing fear, grief, anger, sadness, or something else . . . it's okay. You're a human being. Be human. As long as you don't hurt yourself or anyone else, you have the right to feel whatever you're feeling.

2. **Accept what you cannot change.** We don't choose for bad things to happen to our families. But pushing back against things that we have no power to change gets us nowhere. It just creates tension inside of us and in the family. We don't have to like what's happened, but the sooner we realize that we can't change it, the sooner we can move past difficult events.

3. **Remember it's not your fault.** People affected by divorce, loss, addiction, and other major family changes often feel some responsibility for what's happened. It's important not to blame yourself. Other people's actions and situations beyond your control are not your responsibility. Anyone who says otherwise is wrong.

4. **Talk to someone you trust.** Talking can't change what happened, but knowing that someone else gets it can make a huge difference. If others in your family are too upset, respect that and reach out to someone else. A teacher or counselor may be better able to hear what you have to say. If you feel like there's really no one listening, call 1-800-999-9999 (the Nineline). People there can help you get through this.

No one knows exactly how anything in life will turn out. That's part of the adventure. Part of the challenge is picking yourself up after you've been knocked down. Moving forward begins with accepting what's beyond your control and concentrating on what you can do to make things better. You don't have to let whatever's happened hold you back. Even if things are not the way you wish they were now, they'll change. You can count on that. Until they do, focus on what's right in your life, including the people who are there for you.

Tips for Moving Forward

1. **Keep doing what you love.** Just because something's changed in your life doesn't mean that everything has to. Stick with the activities you've always enjoyed. Maybe it's a sport you play or a favorite hobby. These are the kinds of fun things that can connect us with other people and make us feel good about ourselves.

2. **Take care of yourself.** With heavy family stuff going on, it's sometimes easy to forget that our bodies still need healthy food, relaxation, and sleep. This could be the perfect time to get into a new exercise routine. Whether it's walking, biking, or another activity you enjoy, a regular workout can help you feel better.

3. **Get support from friends.** You may not want people to know about what happened. On the other hand, letting close friends in on the truth may help you get some support and end the need to hide what's going on. If you're not sure you should tell a friend, make two lists. On one, list all the reasons to tell about your family situation. On the other, list all the reasons for not telling. When you're done, see which makes the

most sense. Even if you decide not to tell, you can always change your mind later if you want.

4. **Communicate with the person you miss.** Send him or her a letter, even if writing isn't your thing. If the person you're missing has passed away or can't be reached for whatever reason, you can still think about what you'd like to say and write it down. Putting your feelings into words, whether you get a reply or not, helps you sort things out and take charge of your life. If you're unsure whether it's a good idea to get in touch with the person, you might try the two-list exercise from #3 or talk with someone you trust.

5. **Spend time together as a family.** Tough times at home are easier to deal with when the people in a family stick together. Family meals and activities give everyone a chance to talk about what's happened and get updates and questions answered. Talking about everyday stuff, like what happened at school or work, can also help family members stay connected and moving forward in their lives.

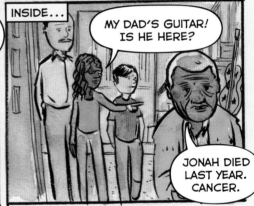

What has happened in the past is unchangeable. It is what it is. That's reality. Even if someone you love is gone from your life now (and maybe forever), you are still connected to your family. That's reality, too. When you rely on the people at home who are still there for you, you keep your connection strong and move together into the future.

Something else about family connections: They may go broader and deeper than you realize. For example, you might reach out to relatives you don't live with—including grandparents, aunts, uncles, cousins, and so on. They can play a big part in your life, too. And since families are always growing (through marriages, births, remarriages), you may discover some very cool relatives you didn't know you had. In the case of cousins, you might even gain some new friends.

From the "COOL FAMILY" FILES

"My aunt and uncle let us live there after we had a house fire, and I know they would do anything for us."
—Frank, 14

"My cousin is like my best friend. He always sticks up for me. I know he's got my back and he knows, no matter what, he can count on me."
—Len, 13

"My stepdad plays Monopoly with me. He thinks about others before himself most times and he is super funny. He and I joke around a lot."
—Estaban, 13

"My mom always knows when I want a hug."
—Sylvie, 13

"Sometimes I miss living with my mom, even though that wasn't always so great. But my foster parents are awesome. They're very loving and they really listen when I talk to them."
—Rochelle, 12

"The best thing about my great-uncle is the goodness of his heart, and the way he appreciates everything having grown up in a poor family. He's had to work since he was about 10."
—Marcus, 12

"My grandpa is pretty much blind, but he's smart. He has hearing problems as well. I especially love how he always tries to be involved with my sister and me, even though it's pretty hard for him."
—Alyce, 11

COLLECTING
Life Stories

Knowing your family history is a great way to connect. That's true whether you want to honor the memory of someone who has died, feel closer to those who may be far away, or simply appreciate your family. Talking to parents and grandparents and other family elders about the past can be as interesting as a book or a movie. Their life stories can also help you understand them and yourself. Try this:

Old photographs. Sit down with a family photo album and an older relative. You can learn a lot by asking simple questions like: Where was this picture taken? Who is that? How old were you then? What did you like to do when you were my age?

Memorabilia. Sports trophies, scrapbooks, vacation souvenirs, and military medals have stories connected to them. If you're interested in hearing their stories, your relatives will probably enjoy telling them.

Saved treasures from childhood. If the older generation saved dolls, toys, games, or books from their childhood, chances are that they have memories attached to them. Ask and you're likely to get a cool story.

Family tree. This is a chart that shows each generation of a family and everyone in it. If your family already has one, ask someone to explain it to you. (Looking at old photos at the same time can help you make connections.) If you don't yet have a family tree, making one could be a fun project for you and a parent or grandparent.

Need to Know?

How Ya Like Me Now by **Brendan Halpin**. Eddie and Alex are cousins, but that doesn't mean they know or like each other. So when Eddie's mom goes into rehab and Eddie moves in with Alex and his parents, it's really weird. But nothing's weirder for Eddie than Alex's school — it's as different from his old school as any two places could be. How can he possibly fit in there?

It's My Life—Family
www.pbskids.org/itsmylife/family
This Web site has information that can help families get along better and rally together during tough times. Visit for advice on how you and the people in your family can make your connections stronger.

Whether you live with a single parent, a grandparent, an aunt or uncle, or a foster parent, you have a family. So don't let anyone tell you anything different.

Sometimes really serious events shake a family to its core. They may even change who is still in the family and who isn't. Those kinds of challenges can test you. They can also offer opportunities to grow. While things may never be the way they used to, you can be proud of the fact that you're moving forward with your life.

Some siblings have an easy relationship and seem to enjoy hanging out. Others may find it really challenging to keep the peace. Even if you get along with sibs most of the time, there are probably moments when you do and say things that get on each other's nerves. That's normal, but when you're in the middle of one of those "here we go again" battles, it's usually not much fun.

Unlike friends, you don't get to choose the people in your family. So you're forced to deal with their personalities, habits, moods, and attitudes. And sometimes, even when siblings aren't actually doing anything annoying, just having them in your space can make you a little crazy.

No brothers or sisters? You didn't choose that either. But keep reading to learn how to get along better with stepsiblings, half-siblings, cousins, or other relatives who—like it or not—you have to spend time with.

From the "Most Annoying" Files

"I don't get my dad's family. When my cousin messes with me he doesn't get in trouble, but when I mess with him, I get yelled at."
—Nicholas, 11

"My big sister is hanging out with the wrong friends and she ends up coming home all cranky. Then my whole family gets in a fight and I end up going to bed with a migraine."
—Christine, 12

"My brother won't let me talk to guys who aren't Vietnamese."
—Mai, 13

"I hate when my sister acts like she's better than everyone else. She likes to control things."
—Les, 14

"My little brother just wants me to hang out with him all the time. If I ignore him he just tags along anyway."
—Philip, 13

"In my stepfather's eyes, my half-brother is perfect. He plays sports and is always home, sucking up. I don't want to change the way I am for my stepdad to like me but I feel that is the only thing that I can do."
—Consuela, 12

My Sibling . . .

1. embarrasses me in front of my friends. **T or F**

2. reads my email. **T or F**

3. gets me in trouble with family adults. **T or F**

4. tries to prove that he/she is better than me in everything. **T or F**

5. teases me or makes rude comments. **T or F**

6. takes my stuff without asking. **T or F**

7. totally controls my parents. **T or F**

8. acts like she/he is the only one in the family who counts. **T or F**

9. starts all the arguments. **T or F**

10. is so immature. **T or F**

If you got:

7–10 True answers. Sounds like you have some real challenges. Instead of continuing to get your buttons pushed, calmly explain to the adults in your family what's going on and how you feel about it. Maybe they'll help negotiate a truce. You can also try calling a family meeting (see page 86).

4–6 True answers. Seems like you have a sibling who can really annoy you. For a better relationship, catch him or her doing something right. For example, if he or she asks to borrow something instead of just taking it, you might say, "It's cool that you asked. So yeah, you can borrow it." It may seem lame, but it actually works!

0–3 True answers. Congratulations! It sounds like you hit the sibling jackpot. Your sister or brother probably feels the same way about you, too. Keep the lines of communication open and you are likely to remain close your entire lives.

When Siblings Are
Being a Pain

1. **Know your buttons.** What are the usual insults you hear? For example, "You eat like a pig." "You're such an idiot." You get the idea. Make a list. Now think about when you're most likely to hear these comments. Knowing what and when can put you on red alert so you can expect it and stop falling into the same trap of overreacting.

2. **Ask: "Why does it get to me?" Hearing "Your face is purple!" probably wouldn't push you over the edge because you know it's not true.** But if, for example, insults about your weight or your intelligence bug you, maybe it's because you put yourself down in similar ways. Just knowing that can help you disconnect the wiring so you don't lose your cool as often.

3. **See it for what it is.** Nobody likes insults. They're purposely chosen to bring you down, but you don't have to let them. When you see the insult for what it really is (just words), it's less likely to get to you.

4. **Shield yourself.** Sunscreen blocks most of the sun's harmful UV rays. So imagine putting on some sib-screen so that you have a shield against insults. That way irritating words thrown in your direction won't have as much power to burn you.

5. **Refuse to play the game.** If whatever's going on between you and a sibling, stepsibling, or cousin has gotten really old, put an end to it. You can do it. Tell yourself, "I've had enough!" Then stop reacting to the button-pushing. And make sure you quit your side of it, too.

Because a sibling relationship (just like any other kind) is a two-way street, both people have a hand in how things are going. The good times are good because of what you both do for each other and the way you talk to each other. When the relationship hits a rough spot, it's never just one person's doing.

Whether you're the oldest child in your family, the youngest, or somewhere in between, nobody is 100 percent responsible for a conflict. And no one gets an automatic free pass. When relationships between siblings or stepsiblings turn rocky it's because both people are doing and saying things that aren't helpful. **(Two-way street, remember?)**

Yeah, Sometimes I'm Annoying Too . . .

"When I tell my cousin that he should do his homework instead of wasting his time, he tells me that I'm really bothering him."
—Julee, 14

"Sometimes I take candy from my stepbrother's drawer. And when he asks me if I did it, I pretend I don't know what he's talking about. Does that count as being annoying?"
—Mike, 11

"A lot of times I let my anger out on my cousin because he's such a sweet guy. I really don't mean to, but I don't know how to stop."
—Dolores, 13

"My older brother likes giving me advice about my ex. If I don't want to hear what he says, I can be rude."
—Ishmael, 13

"My brother says I am a nagger and the most annoying person he has ever met. He gets mad when I won't stop talking."
—Estrella, 12

"When I get really stressed, I yell at my stepsister and hurt her feelings—even if she didn't do anything to me."
—Ben, 13

"When my brother gets annoying I snap at him."
—Lissa, 12

THE INSIDE SCOOP
on Sib Order

Depending on your family, there may be pros and cons to being the oldest, youngest, or in the middle.

Oldest

Pros: Parents often treat the oldest a little more like an adult. That might include staying up later and doing things that younger siblings can't. Sometimes adults in the family put the oldest in charge.

Cons: Some parents expect the oldest child to be super-responsible. They might expect them to do more chores, keep younger siblings out of trouble, and show what "good" behavior looks like.

Middle

Pros: Parents are often less strict with a middle child. Also, having an older brother or sister as a mentor or protector can be a good thing. With at least one older and one younger sib, middle children may learn important life lessons about getting along with people of all ages.

Cons: Because a middle child isn't the oldest or the "baby," he or she may sometimes feel the need to compete for attention. This can create some pressure for the middle kid to stand out and figure out a special role in the family.

Youngest

Pros: The youngest child may get some special attention from the adults and the older kids. He or she might get more freedom to do things than older siblings could do at the same age. Also the youngest child may get less pressure to be "perfect" and more space to be creative and to do his or her own thing.

Cons: Like it or not, the youngest is often the "baby" of the family who gets away with things. Even if the youngest is responsible, some family members may always think of him or her as the "baby."

It's hard to imagine brothers, sisters, stepsiblings, and others at home getting along with one another 100 percent of the time. In real life, you and the people you live with probably are cool with each other sometimes. And other times . . . not so much. But the family bond you share may actually be stronger than you think. And when a sibling, cousin, or someone else in your family really needs help, you're probably there for each other.

My Family Needed Me . . .

"People teased my brother daily and it was stressful for him to go to school and put up with the hassle. One day I told off this kid and he stopped bullying my brother."
—Bailey, 13

"My stepbrother was going nuts about his science project, so I helped him calm down and did the typing for him. It was cool because it made us closer. Now if I need some help, I know I can ask him."
—Zoe, 14

"This guy was picking on my cousin and I stood up for him. The guy ended up hitting me and I defended myself. Both of us got suspended but I wrote a long letter to the administration and they took it off my record."
—Sam, 13

"When someone offered me and my stepsister some drugs, I said no and pulled her away."
—Tanya, 14

"When someone made fun of my cousin's hOaircut, I told her that she was a really nice person. That's more important than what your hair looks like."
—Beth, 13

"My brother almost got run over by a car, and I yelled and stopped the driver."
—Walter, 14

"I stood up for my sister when her friends were at our house and acting nasty. I don't always do that and sometimes I regret not saying something."
—Gillian, 14

Need to Know?

I Am the Wallpaper **by Mark Peter Hughes.** Thirteen-year-old Floey Packer, jealous of her attractive and popular older sister, shares a home with two younger cousins. These people all play a role in a summer vacation full of embarrassing events, but Floey herself is the star.

Siblings: You're Stuck with Each Other, So Stick Together **by James J. Crist and Elizabeth Verdick.** Siblings can definitely get on each other's nerves. Check out this book for practical ways to steer clear of arguments and get along better with sisters, brothers, stepsiblings, cousins, or any others you live with at home.

If you've ever felt that you have the most annoying brother, sister, stepsibling, or cousin in the world, you're not alone. Lots of people feel that way. There may even be someone in your family who sometimes feels that way about you!

But at the end of the day—as annoying as the people you share a home with can be—you are all part of the same family. **Just remembering that can help you get through rough times.**

Chapter 8: Let's Call a Truce

If someone in your family really needs help, doing your part is the top priority. When you're in emergency mode, any bad feelings you may have from recent conflicts often seem to vanish. Something bigger than petty arguments takes over and helps you focus your mind and your actions. That bigger "something" is family loyalty.

WE ARE ALL IN THIS FAMILY

"You look after your family no matter what it takes."
—Eli, 12

"My family means everything to me. So I put my trust in them. That includes my aunts and uncles, my cousins, and my grandparents. Friends are almost like family to me, but sometimes they can spill something out. But I can tell my family anything."
—Shih-Wei, 13

"Family members don't betray or lie to each other. They forgive one another and are always there when you need them."
—April, 11

"Family comes first—even before grades and friends."
—Noelle, 12

"I talk to my mom and stepdad about anything because I love them and trust them to really care about me."
—Brenda, 14

"Whoever is family to you, they are there for you all the time—even when you have no friends you can rely on."
—Nathan, 14

"With your family, you always have someone you can confide your troubles to."
—Tyler, 13

"Stick by your family no matter what the circumstances are, and don't betray them in any way by lying. Love them no matter what."
—Perry, 11

What's Your
NEXT Move?

When there's a situation in your family—either because of a conflict, a sudden change, or an emergency where someone needs help—the best thing to do is think things through and decide what's really going to help. Try this:

1. **Ask yourself: What would improve this situation? Sometimes you might think a conflict would instantly resolve itself if only the other person would change.** That might help, but that's not the whole story. Besides, you can't make anyone change, you can only change your own attitude and behavior. So ask the question again and put yourself into the answer.

2. **It has to start with you.** If there's a conflict that you had a hand in, how have you contributed to things going downhill? What can you do or stop doing that might turn this around? If you didn't contribute to a conflict, you might still play a positive role by answering this question: What could you do to help others make the peace? List your ideas.

3. **Make a plan.** Choose at least one thing from your list and figure out how you're going to make that change. Need some suggestions? Support? Talk to someone else in your family or a trusted friend.

4. **Actually do it.** You say you want changes in your family, so take your idea out of your head and off the page and bring it into the real world. Good luck!

When you do the right thing you gain maturity in the eyes of the adults in your family. What is the right thing?

That depends on what the choices are, but it's often about watching your behavior and keeping your agreements—including being where you say you're going to be and checking in when you're supposed to. It also means being considerate of other people's feelings. All of that is going to score you major points with parents, stepparents, grandparents, and other family members.

Keep adding to those points and you're going to get along better with everyone in your family. That's worth something. You can probably also count on more trust, more respect, more independence, and fewer arguments.

GETTING
ON THE SAME PAGE

"My parents praise me for being responsible when I have been really careful or done something helpful around the house that they didn't expect me to do."
—Connor, 12

"I live with my grandparents and I can talk with them about problems. They explain to me what thought process they're going through when they discipline me."
—Toni, 13

"The only thing that I would change about my family is to perhaps have them guilt me less. If I do something wrong, I'm likely to know it from my inner voice. They don't need to rub it in. Other than that, I'm good with them."
—Teri, 13

"My parents kept complaining that I was spending too much time on the computer, even if it's just checking my email or reading about something on the Web. But they never really said how much time was okay. After we agreed on exact amounts of time for weekdays and weekends, we don't fight about that anymore."
—Lee, 11

"Both my parents are police, so there was this time when my mom had to interview a man whose car had been in an accident. It turned out their son was the boy driving. My parents told me how proud they are of me because they know I would never do anything like that!"
—James, 14

Family Meetings

If you'd rather clean the bathroom than have a "family meeting," hold on a sec. It's not as bad as it sounds. In fact, they can actually be okay. A family meeting is just a chance to talk in a calm and respectful way so everyone can have their say. (Let's hear it for democracy!) Family meetings are also about understanding each other's feelings and behavior and finding better ways to resolve conflicts. (More peace at home! How can that be bad?) Anyone can call a family meeting. Here's how:

Step #1: Schedule a meeting. Sure, everyone is busy, but don't give up. If you really try, you can find a time when the whole family can sit down together.

Step #2: Create ground rules. You just need three simple rules:

— **Agree that one person talks at a time.** When he or she talks, everyone shows respect by listening.

— **Agree not to interrupt.** You deserve respect and so does everyone else. If anyone interrupts, the speaker can calmly say, "Excuse me. I am talking."

— **Agree to stay focused on the topic at hand.** Don't bring up past problems. That only adds stress and may make people defensive.

Step #3: Put your feelings into words. Use "I" statements, as in: "I feel _____ when you _____." For example, "I feel frustrated when you don't let me IM my friends" or "I feel angry when you tell me what to do." When you stick with your own feelings, instead of words like "You always . . ." or "You never . . ." others are more likely to listen because no one's blaming them for anything.

Step #4: Make a plan. It takes at least two people to get into a conflict. To figure out your part, ask yourself:

— **What did I do or say that got the other person upset?**

— **What could I have done differently?**

— **Next time, what can I try instead?**

Family meetings can also be used to talk about good stuff, like remembering special times you've had with your family over the years or planning for an event. Getting together regularly to talk and listen may help you appreciate the good part that your family plays in your life.

From the "Family Traditions" FILES

"Every Christmas, my family from the city comes up here. We have lots of food, make jokes, play video games, and have so much fun. There's a video camera running the whole time, and we always have a good laugh!"
—Sam, 13

"For Thanksgiving, we all travel to the United States for a visit to my cousins, grandparents, aunts, and uncles. Even though Canada and the United States have different days for the holiday, we find some time to spend together and have a fantastic dinner."
—Jeanne, 11

"On the Fourth of July, we go camping and we watch fireworks."
—Bernard, 11

"Since my mom is from back east, the whole family watches the ball drop in Times Square on New Year's Eve and counts down till midnight. And we have apple cider."
—Marc, 14

"For Halloween we have pumpkin-shaped pizza, get in our costumes, have a photo op, then go trick-or-treating. Mom or Dad takes turns staying at home handing out candy and coming with us. After, my sis and I go through our candy and trade stuff."
—Claire, 11

"During the holidays we start off with a delicious dinner, each year has different food. All the teens and the kids around my age are really hyper and excited! We have separate tables—one for the teens and kids and another for all the adults. We can talk about school, or maybe even how funny our parents are!"
—Robin, 12

"The family tradition I love most is Bikin seriki. In English it is 'King's party.' This is done yearly because my grandfather is a king in my village in Kenya. There I see a lot of traditional dances and attires."
—Jomo, 14

"On birthdays, we always go to the birthday person's favorite restaurant and they get their dessert with a candle on it."
—Chaz, 12

Need to Know?

The Bright Side: Surviving Your Parents' Divorce by Max Sindell. Divorce, separation, remarriage, and other family transitions can be overwhelming. That doesn't mean, though, that they have to be bad. This book shows that with a positive attitude, tough situations in families can actually end up in better times for everyone involved.

Forever Rose by Hilary McKay. It's a few weeks before Christmas and Rose feels like she's the only one in her family who even notices that the house is empty most of the time. Do they care that it's the time of year when "family" is really supposed to mean something?

If you're like most teens, there are probably moments when you just don't appreciate your family very much and they don't appreciate you. That can happen when you feel like parents are giving you a hard time and you push back, or when you and your siblings just are not getting along. Or a million other reasons. But when the storm clouds pass and whatever was going on is behind you, you may be left with a feeling that your family is okay. And you know something? They really are.

Index

About the Author

Annie Fox, M.Ed., graduated from Cornell University with a degree in Human Development and Family Studies and completed her master's in Education at the State University of New York at Cortland. After a few years teaching in the classroom, computers changed her life and she began to explore the ways in which technology could be used to empower teens.

Annie has since contributed to many online projects, including as creator, designer, and writer for the The InSite—a Web site for teens taking on life's challenges. Annie also answers questions for the Hey Terra! feature, an online advisor. Her Internet work has contributed to the publication of multiple books, including *Too Stressed to Think?* and the Middle School Confidential series. Annie is available for public speaking engagements and workshop presentations on teen and parenting issues.

When not answering Hey Terra! letters, Annie enjoys yoga, meditation, cooking, hiking, traveling, and, most of all, spending time with her husband David and the rest of the family.

About the Illustrator

Matt Kindt was born in 1973 to a pair of artistically supportive parents. Living briefly in New York, Matt has spent most of his years in the Midwest, and the last 15 years in Webster Groves, Missouri, a suburb of St. Louis. In middle school, he would often create mini-comics featuring the teachers, to the delight of his fellow classmates. Matt is the Harvey Award–winning writer and artist of the graphic novels *Super Spy* and *2 Sisters* and co-creator of the Pistolwhip series. He has been nominated for four Eisner and three Harvey Awards. In addition to graphic novels, Matt also works as a freelance illustrator and graphic designer. When he is not working, Matt enjoys long trips to the playground with his wife and daughter.

Fast, Friendly, and Easy to Use
www.freespirit.com

Browse the catalog

Info & extras

Many ways to search

Quick check-out

Stop in and see!

1.800.735.7323 • fax 612.337.5050 • help4kids@freespirit.com

FOLLOW THE JOURNEY OF JACK, JEN, CHRIS, ABBY, MATEO, AND MICHELLE—SIX STUDENTS JUST TRYING TO FIGURE IT ALL OUT IN MIDDLE SCHOOL . . .

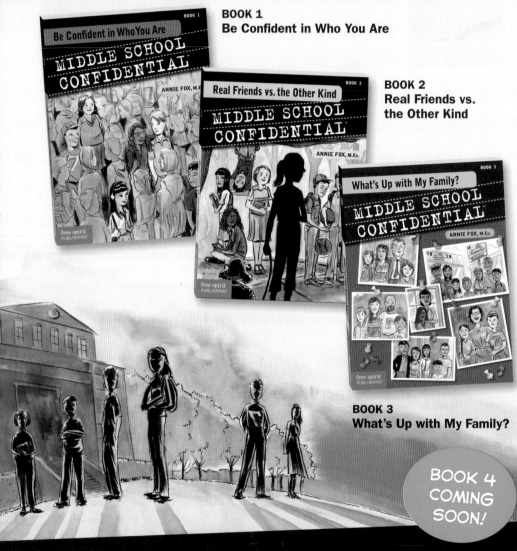

BOOK 1
Be Confident in Who You Are

BOOK 2
Real Friends vs. the Other Kind

BOOK 3
What's Up with My Family?

BOOK 4 COMING SOON!

The Middle School Confidential™ series blends fiction and practical advice in a contemporary, graphic-novel format that will draw in even reluctant readers. Includes quizzes, quotes from real kids, tips, tools, and resources. For ages 11–14.